CW01072296

Margaret Roberts

◆ LITTLE BOOK OF ◆

BASIL

ISBN 1 86812 671 4

First edition, first impression 1997

Published by Southern Book Publishers (Pty) Ltd
PO Box 3103, Halfway House, 1685

Design and DTP by Tracey Mackenzie
Set in 10 on 12 point Palatino
Illustrations by Margaret Roberts
Printed and bound by National Book Printers,
Drukkery Street, Goodwood, Western Cape

Contents

Origins of basil, the king of herbs

Of all the herbs basil's king.
For all the healing it can bring,
for taste and fragrance praises sing;
basil's good for everything!

The Greek word for basil, *basileus*, meaning 'king', is an indication of the reverence and respect with which this remarkable herb has been held through the ages.

Basil originated in India and tropical Asia, where it was also considered to be the king of herbs, and has been offered through the ages in reverence to the Hindu gods Krishna and Vishnu.

In the gardens of Rome at the time of the Caesars, basil was allocated extensive space, and from there it was taken to France and Britain. From Europe it spread widely and quickly to the Americas and Africa. Each country to which it was introduced developed its own recipes and medicines, some of which were recorded as far back as the sixteenth century.

Today basil is farmed extensively throughout the world and the many varieties of the herb are often confusing in their origins and nomenclature.

Growing basil

All varieties of basil need full sun and rich, well-composted, well-drained soil. Generally basil is a tender herb, which is why many growers treat it — even the prolific perennial varieties — as an annual, except in tropical and sub-tropical frost-free areas.

Owing to its deep tap root and lateral root system, basil does not like to be moved, so set out seedlings in moist soil in a hole filled with water, in the place where they are to remain, no less than 40 cm apart.

Because basil is used for culinary as well as cosmetic and medicinal purposes, it is important that it is organically grown. The soil should be well composted with organic, unsprayed materials and never sprayed with anything other than a natural herbal insecticide (see page 58).

Seeds can be sown in spring in protected seed trays filled with river sand and transplanted to their permanent positions when the plants are about 6 cm high. Keep them moist and well shaded for the first few days while they establish themselves. Thereafter a twice-weekly watering is enough. I find a substantial mulch around their roots keeps them sturdy and vigorous, particularly in the summer heat, as it helps to retain moisture and control weeds.

Varieties of basil

❧

There are about 150 varieties of basil in the world today. Like all the Labiates (this great family includes the mints, rosemaries and sages), they cross-pollinate readily, and every country has its own varieties within varieties. A daunting task confronts the botanists in the naming and description of these varieties and often one finds that affectionate, descriptive names rule the confusion.

At least 15 varieties are easily available in South Africa, including our own indigenous basils, Transvaal basil (*Ocimum canum*), Zulu basil (*O. urticifolium*) and the stately camphor basil (*Basilicum kilimandscharicum*) which originated on the lower slopes of Mount Kilimanjaro but now grows wild all over Africa.

Annual basils

These are probably the best known of all the basils and are easily propagated from seed. They form the bulk of the gourmet or cook's garden and have a short life from September through to the first frosts in May, even in tropical areas, when they become weak and straggly, serving only to be dumped on the compost heap or turned into insect-repelling sprays.

Sweet basil

SWEET BASIL *Ocimum basilicum*

Sweet basil and the larger-leaved Italian basil can be easily cultivated from seed in trays in spring, and the seedlings can be planted out after all danger of frost has passed.

It forms a neat bush up to 60 cm in height and from mid-summer onwards is covered in white flowers that are much loved by bees and butterflies. The leaves are rich in oils and just brushing past the bush will release its clove-like minty freshness. Sweet basil is a prolific annual, and responds well to picking — literally the more you pick the more leaves it will produce.

Where a recipe calls for basil in cookery books across the world, the annual sweet basils, including the large Italian basil, are the ones to use.

MINIATURE GREEK OR BUSH BASIL
Ocimum basilicum minimum

This lovely, tiny-leaved, 20 cm high bush is sometimes called 'spicy globe'. It is an excellent basil to grow in poor conditions. In the hot, sandy soil on the northern slopes of the Magaliesberg, where I live, this compact little bush has withstood long periods of drought and searing winds that have scorched the leaves of other basil varieties.

The flowers set in late autumn and by the following spring masses of seed has dropped which germinates all around the place where the mother plant has stood. I transplant these with ease in late spring.

Its compact shape makes bush basil an excellent pot plant for full sun, although in a pot it would need considerably more water.

Although it does not have the intense flavour of sweet basil, it is nevertheless a wonderful addition to tomato dishes, pasta and pizza.

Miniature Greek basil

Dark Opal Basil *Ocimum basilicum purpurascens*

Exquisitely dark and exotic looking, this decorative basil grows to between 30 and 60 cm in height, has a rich, clove-like scent, deeply serrated leaves and bright pink flowers. The flavour is not as strong as that of the true sweet basils, but it looks so pretty on salads and savoury dishes that I find myself using it more and more. It looks wonderful as an edging to the spinach bed and with its dark maroon foliage it looks most attractive planted between other showy annuals.

I use this basil to make bath and hair rinse vinegars (see page 47) because of its beautiful deep ruby colour.

I love its leaves finely chopped over avocado and feta cheese salads, and add whole leaves and flowers to vinegar with a teaspoon or two of celery seed to make a delicious salad dressing.

Dark opal basil seed readily germinates and must be planted out in full sun in late September, as it is particularly frost tender.

&• HANDY HINT
Basil makes an excellent pot plant but needs a big deep pot and full sun.

GREEN RUFFLES *Ocimum basilicum* hybrid

I have tried growing this new variety of basil in the Herbal Centre gardens and in spite of drought, heat and all the other adverse conditions, it did extremely well, which just goes to show that the Labiatae family don't like wet feet and thrive in heat!

The large leaves are very deeply serrated and remain half closed. The bush is neat, compact and prolific — the more you pick, the more it grows. In drought conditions my plants didn't reach 40 cm in height, but possibly in rich, well-watered soil the bush would grow considerably taller and wider than 40 cm.

The leaves are not as tender or as strong as the ordinary basils, but nevertheless added to salsas and sauces and for face steamers, I found them excellent.

❧ HANDY HINT
In midsummer, layer leaves of sweet basil and coarse salt in a crock and store in a cool place for use in the winter months.

LEMON BASIL *Ocimum basilicum citriodorum*

This miniature variety of basil has recently been introduced to South Africa. It seems to thrive on neglect, making it an excellent variety for waterwise gardening and dry, hot areas.

It is a compact bush, about 30 cm high, though not as neat as *O.b. minimum*. Like bush basil, lemon basil makes an excellent pot plant for full sun although in pots it does need watering twice daily. Fill the pots with rich compost mixed into good potting soil for a full season of lavish pickings. I use a large pot 30 cm in diameter to last the full season and each year I plant new seedlings in completely fresh new soil. In midsummer I add a spadeful of compost to give the plants a boost and find that I'm still picking young tender leaves right through autumn.

With its distinctive lemon scent and flavour, this basil is most appealing in any number of dishes and cosmetics.

Whole bushes placed indoors in tubs of water will keep mosquitoes out on hot summer nights and rubbing kitchen counter tops with the crushed branches keeps them fly-free. I rub them onto the dogs too, with the result that there seem to be no fleas. I'll use it in future as a companion plant for my strawberries and red cherry tomatoes.

Lemon basil

CINNAMON BASIL *Ocimum basilicum* species

The origins of cinnamon basil are uncertain, but it is believed to have come from America, and it was originally referred to as 'cultivated basil'. It reaches a height of up to 60 cm and is bushy in growth with lovely magenta and pink flowers, small leaves and a distinctive taste and smell reminiscent of cinnamon and cloves.

It can be difficult to find, but seeds are becoming more readily available. Like the ordinary basils it is a quick annual. It needs full sun and well-dug and well-composted light soil. Plants should be spaced at least 70 cm apart to allow room for the bushy growth. It grows easily and true to type (although the magenta colour may go greenish) from seed collected from the bush at season's end.

Its cinnamon-like fragrance and taste complement sweet dishes and drinks and will add a new dimension to a beetroot salad. It is particularly attractive in lemon colddrinks — a leaf or two and a flowering tip give a delicious flavour. The flowering heads with their dark pink stems are lovely in dried flower arrangements.

Cinnamon basil

LIQUORICE BASIL AND SPICY BASIL *Ocimum* species

Liquorice basil and spicy basil are two fairly new varieties that have very distinctive flavours. They are both species of *Ocimum* with pink and maroon flowering stalks that dry beautifully for the vase, bringing in their distinctive aniseed or clove-like fragrance to scent a whole room. They are pretty as annuals, but also make excellent companion plants to keep aphids off spinach and lettuce.

Strong in flavour, I have used finely chopped fresh leaves very sparingly with cream cheese, avocado pear and stewed peaches, and have found the aniseed-clove taste perfect in all these dishes.

An Italian chef I know singes freshly chopped leaves in hot oil before stir frying mushrooms or green peppers and the taste is simply wonderful.

❧ HANDY HINT
Crushed basil leaves placed on windowsills and in bowls will freshen a whole room.

Perennial basils

There are several perennial basils available, and much confusion exists, even amongst botanists, as to the identity of the various hybrids. Perennial basils are best for room fresheners and insect sprays rather than cooking, owing to their pungent scent.

For all perennial basils, take cuttings of no more than 6 cm in length and tear off the little sprigs, leaving a small heel. Strip off the lower leaves, nip off the top bud and press the cutting into wet sand, keeping it shaded and moist until little roots have formed. Then carefully transplant the cutting into a pot of good soil to strengthen. Before planting it out, harden the plant by placing the pot in the sun for lengthening periods, never allowing it to dry out, to make the plant wilt resistant when it is finally planted out in full sun in the garden.

CAMPHOR BASIL *Ocimum kilimandscharicum*

Pungent, shrubby and prolific, this beautiful basil originates from the lower slopes of Mount Kilimanjaro. In the garden in full sun the bush grows to about 1 m in height and width and is a mass of flowers all year round, even in the coldest months. Although it is frost tender and needs protection during winter, it is probably the hardiest of all the basils.

It benefits from being clipped back hard, and the bush seems to respond by filling out. I shape it well in midwinter to prepare for the new burst of shoots and flowers in early spring. Grown as a hedge planted closely together, camphor basil really comes into its own. It can be clipped or left to flower freely as is its charming habit, and the haze of bees, moths and butterflies hovering over it is a glorious sight.

I grow camphor basil in a big tub on the patio in full sun as a mosquito repellent. Merely crush the leaves in passing to release the camphor-like fragrance and mosquitoes and flies flee! I cut long sprays of flowering branches for the vase in summer to keep flies out of the house. Crushed camphor basil leaves will freshen a smoke-filled room and some African tribes burn the sticks and seed heads to clear the air if anyone is sick. Other tribes burn it and inhale the smoke for coughs, colds and chest ailments.

Camphor basil

PERENNIAL WHITE BASIL *Ocimum basilicum* hybrid

Similar in every way to perennial pink basil, this cross-pollinated basil hybridised at the Herbal Centre basil garden about 10 years ago. The differences are its white flowers, pale green stems and bracts, shiny leaves and bushy growth. The white basil is perhaps not as prolific as the pink variety, but it is simply charming!

It has the same uses as the pink perennial basil and is equally frost tender. It looks superb in a big pot that can be wheeled onto a sheltered patio for the winter.

> ❧ HANDY HINT
> Wrap basil leaves around fruit that does not ripen, keep it warm and it will soon be ready to eat.

PERENNIAL PINK BASIL *Ocimum basilicum* hybrid

This variety of basil cross pollinated here at the Herbal Centre, and I couldn't live without it! Its parentage is hazy, but it is probably derived from camphor basil, while its dark stems, wine coloured bracts and pale pink flowers would seem to connect it with dark opal basil. Its leaves are a bright shiny green (those of camphor basil are dull grey-green) and its growth habit is prolific yet dainty, tender yet robust in its profusion of flowers. It forms a neater, rounder bush than camphor basil and yet never quite reaches the same 1 m in height, except where it has a lot of water.

I've grown it as a hedge and find it enchanting as it is literally afloat with butterflies from midsummer onwards. Clipping back is essential to prevent it from becoming thin and straggly and with each pruning it becomes sturdier. Bunches of leaves and flowering sprigs are good fly and mosquito repellents rubbed onto furniture or pets and a few bunches in vases of water will clear the air of odours. Fresh bunches tied and used to swat the legs on balmy summer evenings on the lawn ward off mosquitoes, while the pleasant, clove-like scent banishes heat fatigue and soothes tension headaches.

Perennial pink basil

TULSI OR SACRED BASIL *Ocimum gratissimum, O. sanctum*

This very strongly clove-scented basil has been revered through the centuries in Eastern religious ceremonies and in ayurvedic medicine. Sprigs of it were used to prepare holy water and pots of it were often set at the altar in a church, or used to swear an oath in either a sacred place or in a court of justice. Tulsi is still held in reverence today and I grow it abundantly for the Indian community for particular religious ceremonies.

Most Hindu homes keep a pot of tulsi for its disinfecting properties, to cleanse the air and to protect the family from evil. A basil sprig or leaf is carefully placed on the breast of dead Hindus as an insurance, or pass, to paradise.

Tulsi is different in appearance and growth habit to the other basils. It has dark, lacy flower heads, rich in aroma, and attractive, velvety leaves. Bunches of tulsi look wonderful in summer floral arrangements with agapanthus and hydrangeas, and as a boon they will keep flies and mosquitoes out of the house with their rich, clove-like scent.

Tulsi makes an excellent tub subject. It can be clipped into a neat shape and all the clippings added to pot pourris. Like the other basils it needs frost protection in a very cold winter.

Tulsi

PERENNIAL SWEET BASIL OR 'MARGARET'S FAVOURITE'

This new variety is a freak — a cross that happened to come in a tray of sweet basil seedlings. It is a big and bushy perennial with medium-sized leaves. It benefits from clipping and does need to be staked in windy areas. The flavour of the leaves is pure delicious basil, but its flowering head is not like any other basil. It forms a plume of magenta bracts which do not turn to seed of any description. We have trialled it for six years here at the Herbal Centre, and found it to be everybody's favourite as it can be potted and grown on a sunny stoep out of winter's frost. It also does well in a vase on a kitchen windowsill in sprigs of any length, and the small leaves can be cut or stripped off and new ones form. I've even planted the denuded sprigs and had them burst into leaf. As it ages, the leaves become smaller but are still full of flavour.

If you crave fresh basil all year round, this is the one for you!

'Margaret's favourite'

Cooking
with basil

No cook should be without fresh basil close at hand. In winter when fresh basil is not available, basil oil and vinegar, or basil leaves stored in a crock with alternating layers of salt, come into their own.

Use fresh basil lavishly in salads, soups, sauces, and tomato and vegetable dishes. It is a wonderfully versatile herb, and the more you use it, the more difficult you will find it to be without it!

The annual basils are best for cooking, the most commonly used being the ordinary sweet basil *(Ocimum basilicum)*. Other favourites are dark opal basil, bush basil and lemon basil.

EQUIVALENT MEASUREMENTS

1 teaspoon = 5 ml
1 tablespoon = 12,5 ml
1 cup = 250 ml

Starters

B asil complements vegetables wonderfully well and these tantalising starters or hors d'oeuvres are a perfect way to begin a meal.

BASIL DIP WITH CRUDITÉS

Serves 6–8

This is simply delicious on a hot summer evening with vegetables and fruits in season.

Arrange a platter of carrot, celery and courgette sticks, radishes, baby mealies, button mushrooms, tomato wedges, asparagus spears (either tinned or cooked and then cooled), thin rounds of beetroot, apple wedges and green grapes. In the centre place a glass bowl of basil dip:

1 carton cream cheese
1 carton plain yoghurt
cayenne pepper and sea salt to taste
2 tablespoons basil vinegar
2 tablespoons honey
2 tablespoons finely chopped fresh sweet basil
   (or lemon basil or dark opal basil)

Mix all the ingredients well.

BASIL MUSHROOMS

Serves 4

4-8 large flat brown mushrooms
butter
sea salt and black pepper
2 tablespoons chopped fresh sweet basil leaves
2 cups croutons
lemon wedges

Gently grill the mushrooms with little dabs of butter spread onto them for 4 minutes or until lightly browned and soft. Serve hot, surrounded by croutons and sprinkled with the chopped basil, salt and pepper. Serve with lemon wedges and decorate with a basil leaf.

To make croutons, gently fry brown bread cubes in a little sunflower oil until browned and crisp. Drain on paper towels.

&❦ HANDY HINT
In midsummer, layer leaves of sweet basil and coarse salt in a crock and store in a cool place for use in the winter months.

BASIL AND TOMATO ROLL

Serves 6

3 crusty breadrolls
3 medium-sized tomatoes
1 medium-sized onion
sea salt
black pepper
3 teaspoons brown sugar
1 tablespoon butter
fresh basil, chopped

Cut the breadrolls in half, scoop out the soft inside and crumble. Chop the tomatoes and onion. Sprinkle with a little sea salt, black pepper and brown sugar.

Melt the butter in a non-stick frying pan and quickly brown the breadcrumbs. Remove them from the pan and set aside. Add the tomatoes and onions to the pan and cook until tender.

Mix with the breadcrumbs, spoon into the empty bread roll shells, sprinkle with fresh chopped basil and serve hot in a folded paper serviette. This is real finger food!

BASIL FRITTERS

Serves 4-6

2 cups flour
2 teaspoons baking powder
sea salt and cayenne pepper to taste
½ cup chopped fresh sweet basil leaves
1 cup milk and a little water (to make a fairly thin batter)
sunflower oil

Mix all the ingredients well. Warm a little oil in a frying pan, drop small spoonfuls of the batter into the pan, allow to cook and when little bubbles form, carefully turn over to fry on the other side.

Keep the cooked fritters hot and serve hot with a squeeze of lemon juice.

Soups

Basil adds superb flavour to hot and cold soups. Chop it finely and add it just before serving when its flavour is at its peak.

CREAMED BASIL, LEEK AND CELERY SOUP
Serves 6

50 g butter
1 large head celery, finely chopped
1 large onion, finely chopped
8 leeks, finely sliced
1 litre good chicken stock
150 ml milk
50 g brown flour
freshly ground black pepper and sea salt to taste
150 ml plain yoghurt
2 tablespoons chopped fresh sweet basil

Melt the butter in a saucepan, and add the celery, onion and leeks. Sauté until tender and lightly browned. Add the stock and simmer for 25 minutes.

Purée in a liquidiser and return to the saucepan and heat slowly. Meanwhile mix a little milk with the flour, salt and pepper to make a smooth paste. Gradually add the rest of the milk and the yoghurt. Mix well and add slowly to the purée. Heat until it boils, remove from the stove and add the chopped basil. Serve hot, decorated with a basil leaf and a dusting of nutmeg.

BASIL AND BEETROOT SOUP
Serves 6
Delicious served hot or cold, this variation of borscht can be made well in advance and kept chilled, or served hot.

sunflower oil
3 onions, sliced
½ kg potatoes, peeled and diced
½ kg beetroot, freshly cooked, peeled and diced
a few fresh beetroot leaves, chopped (stalks included)
1-1½ litres good vegetable stock
½ cup fresh sweet basil leaves, finely chopped
1 tablespoon Italian flat-leaved parsley, finely chopped
sea salt and black pepper to taste
juice of 1 fresh lemon
2 wineglasses red wine (optional)
150 ml sour cream

Heat the oil in a saucepan. Sauté the onions and potatoes in the oil, turning frequently. Add the beetroot and cook gently for a few minutes, being careful not to brown the vegetables.

Add the chopped beetroot leaves. Add the stock and bring to the boil. Simmer for 20 minutes. Then liquidise and return to the saucepan and bring to the boil again. Add the chopped basil, parsley, lemon juice, salt and pepper and wine (if desired).

Remove from the heat and pour into warmed bowls. Swirl a little sour cream into each bowl and serve hot.

Alternatively, chill the soup, adding the sour cream once it is cold. Serve with fresh basil and a squeeze of lemon juice.

TOMATO AND BASIL SOUP

Serves 6

This is the perfect summer soup, reminiscent of hot Spanish nights!
Use sun-ripened tomatoes for the best flavour.

little sunflower oil
2 large onions, finely chopped
2 leeks, thinly sliced
2 sticks celery, thinly sliced
2 carrots, peeled and grated
½ kg tomatoes, skinned and roughly chopped
3 tablespoons honey
sea salt and cayenne pepper to taste
1 litre water
½ cup fresh sweet basil, finely chopped
½ cup basil vinegar

Heat a little oil in a large saucepan. Sauté the onions and leeks until
tender and starting to brown. Add the celery and carrots. Fry
gently, while stirring. Add the tomatoes, honey, water and
seasoning. Simmer gently, stirring occasionally, for 20 minutes.

Add the chopped basil and basil vinegar and liquidise
everything together. Chill.

Serve in glass bowls with fresh chopped basil sprinkled over
each one and a dash of cream if desired, and a big bowl of croutons
decorated with basil leaves.

*HINT: To skin the tomatoes, immerse them in boiling water for 10 min-
utes, then rub off the skins.*

Chicken and Basil Soup

Serves 6-8

The spiciness of the basil complements the blandness of the vegetables superbly in this tasty light soup. In winter, when fresh basil is not available, use salted basil or basil vinegar or oil. This is an excellent nurturing soup for flu and colds.

1 large onion, finely chopped
4 celery sticks and leaves, finely sliced
little sunflower oil
2 large carrots, finely grated
2 large potatoes, peeled and diced
2 litres water
1 chicken carcass and leftover gravy (about 1 cup)
juice of 1 lemon
sea salt and cayenne pepper to taste
½ cup fresh sweet basil leaves, chopped
2 sprigs parsley, finely chopped
1 cup cooked brown rice

In a large cast iron pot lightly brown the onions and celery in the sunflower oil. Add the carrots and potatoes and stir fry for 3 minutes. Then add the water, the chicken carcass and gravy, and lemon juice. Simmer for 20-30 minutes or until the vegetables are tender. Remove the chicken bones, add the sea salt and cayenne pepper to taste and the chopped basil, parsley and brown rice. Simmer for a further 2 minutes.

Ladle the soup into hot bowls and serve at once with crusty brown bread spread with basil butter.

Fish dishes

Basil is being used more and more with fish in modern cuisine, which makes good sense when one thinks of how basil helps the digestion of fats, breaks down toxins and enhances the digestive process. These recipes prove that basil and fish are an excellent, if somewhat unconventional, combination.

POTATO AND BASIL FISH CAKES
Serves 4-6

3 cups mashed potato seasoned with cayenne pepper and sea salt
4 cups cooked flaked hake seasoned with salt and fresh lemon juice
2 beaten eggs
½ cup flour
½ cup fresh sweet sweet basil, chopped
2 medium onions, finely chopped
½ cup chives, finely chopped
sunflower oil for frying

Mix all the ingredients, form into patties between two spoons and fry gently in a pan with hot oil. Turn to lightly brown both sides. Drain on absorbent paper. Serve hot with a salad.

Basil and Hake Stir Fry

Serves 4

Easy to make and wonderfully tasty, this is a perfect lunch or supper dish and is complete in 10-15 minutes.

sunflower oil
1 onion, finely chopped
4 frozen hake pieces, deboned and skinned,
and thinly sliced while frozen
little flour
1 large potato, peeled and coarsely grated
1 small tin peas, drained or 1 cup fresh cooked peas
6-8 button mushrooms, thinly sliced
1 cup green outer leaves of cabbage, thinly sliced
juice of 1 lemon
sea salt to taste
freshly ground black pepper
½ cup fresh sweet basil, chopped
1 tablespoon fresh parsley, chopped

Heat a wok or big pan, and add the sunflower oil and onion. Meanwhile thinly slice the hake pieces, roll in the flour and add to the hot oil. Lightly turn and fry and when starting to brown, add the potato, peas, mushrooms and thinly shredded cabbage. Turn gently with a wooden spatula. Add a little lemon juice and the salt and pepper. When tender, sprinkle in the basil, turn once or twice, then spoon into a serving dish and lightly sprinkle with parsley. Serve hot with brown rice.

GRILLED MARINATED FISH WITH BASIL

Serves 4

Marinade
juice of 1 lemon or ½ cup vinegar
½ cup sweet basil, finely chopped
a few pieces of thinly shaved chilli
1 tablespoon crushed coriander seeds
½ cup olive oil
1 teaspoon black pepper
2 teaspoons sea salt

4 pieces of fish, skinned, boned and filleted

Put all the marinade ingredients in a glass jar with a good lid and shake for a minute or two. Place the fish fillets in a shallow dish. Pour the marinade over the fish, cover and place on the lowest shelf of the refrigerator. Every now and then turn the fish so that the marinade penetrates well. Leave overnight if possible. Then grill the fish quickly, browning slightly. Spoon the marinade over the fish while it is grilling. Serve with crusty bread and a salad.

Main dishes

Add basil to beef, mutton and pork dishes, lentils and dried beans, and any dish made with tomato.

BEEFY BASIL BREDIE
Serves 6

1 kg rump steak, cubed and thinly sliced
2 large onions, finely chopped
2 sticks celery, thinly sliced
4 carrots, cut into thin strips
3 large potatoes, diced
1 tablespoon crushed mixed coriander and fennel seeds
juice of 1 lemon
sea salt and black pepper to taste
4 large tomatoes, skinned and chopped
½ cup brown sugar
1 green pepper, thinly chopped
1 litre water
½ cup sweet basil, freshly chopped

Brown the meat and onions in a little oil in a large pot. Add the celery, carrots, potatoes, coriander and fennel seeds, lemon juice, salt and pepper. Turn in the oil. Add the tomatoes, brown sugar, green pepper and water. Turn down the heat. Simmer with the lid on, adding more water if necessary. When tender, add the basil, stir well, and boil for another 2 minutes before serving.

CHICKEN WITH BASIL STUFFING

Serves 6
Served either hot or cold, this is a superb standby.

whole chicken, including giblets and neck
lemon juice
salt and pepper
fresh thyme
4 potatoes, peeled and halved
2 onions, peeled and halved
1 litre water

Stuffing
2 slices brown bread, crumbled
juice of 1 lemon
1 stick celery, finely chopped
1 onion, finely chopped
½ - ¾ cup plain yoghurt
salt and black pepper to taste
2 tablespoons fresh sweet basil, chopped
1 tablespoon fresh parsley, chopped

Mix together the stuffing ingredients. Stuff the cavity of the chicken and place the chicken in a clay pot or cast iron cooker. Sprinkle with lemon juice, salt and pepper and a little fresh thyme. Tuck in the potatoes and onions around the chicken as well as the giblets and neck. Add the water. Bake at 180°C for 2½ hours or until the chicken is tender. Check that it does not dry out, adding more water if necessary (this forms a good gravy). Serve with peas, cauliflower and gem squash.

PORK SAUSAGE AND BASIL GRILL

Serves 4-6

Alongside this tasty braai or grill I often serve brinjals, green peppers and onions brushed with basil oil and a little sea salt.

8-12 pork sausages, split open
1 cup fresh chopped pounded sweet basil, mixed into
½ cup olive oil with 1 tablespoon crushed coriander
cayenne pepper and lemon juice

Lay the sausages cut side up over a hot fire or under the oven grill and spread the basil paste over them. Arrange other vegetables around and grill until lightly browned and well cooked through. Serve hot with a green salad, lemon wedges and mashed potatoes.

MEAT BALLS WITH BASIL SAUCE
Serves 4-6

1 kg lean minced beef
2 onions, finely chopped
2 sticks celery, finely chopped
3 carrots, finely grated
1 apple, peeled and finely grated
1 tablespoon fresh parsley, chopped
2 beaten eggs
sea salt and cayenne pepper to taste
sunflower oil for frying

Sauce
6-8 tomatoes, skinned and chopped
1 large onion, finely chopped
1 green pepper, seeded and finely chopped
3 courgettes, grated
1 tablespoon honey or brown sugar
1 teaspoon crushed coriander seeds
2 tablespoons fresh sweet basil, chopped

Mix all the ingredients for the meat balls together. Press into balls the size of a golf ball, then flatten them. Fry in the oil in a frying pan until nicely browned and well cooked through. Drain on absorbent paper and keep hot in a casserole dish in the oven.

Meanwhile boil up the tomato sauce mixture, leaving out only the chopped basil, which is added last. Mix well and pour over the meat balls.

Serve piping hot with brown rice and a green salad.

Desserts

For desserts the nicest basils to use are camphor basil, perennial pink basil and lemon basil. Their spicy, clove-like flavour goes well with fruit and sweet dishes.

The camphor basils and the perennial spicy basils have the marvellous ability of reducing the need for sweetening in a recipe. So where you use these basils, start by lessening the sugar by a quarter, or perhaps by half, until the taste is to your liking. Use a 15 cm sprig, including the flowering seed head, per recipe as a general guideline.

STEWED FRUIT WITH CAMPHOR BASIL

pears, peaches, plums, quinces or apples (or a combination)
½ cup brown sugar for every 1½ cups fruit
½ cup water for every cup fruit
sprig camphor basil, including seed head

Peel and slice the fruit and sprinkle with brown sugar. Add the water and camphor basil sprig.

Simmer gently with the lid on until the fruit is tender. Remove the basil stalk. Serve hot or cold in glass bowls with whipped cream or custard for a delicious dessert.

SPICY BASIL APPLE CRUMBLE
Serves 6-8

1 kg apples, peeled, cored and diced
½ pineapple, sliced and diced, or 1 small tin pineapple chunks
camphor or perennial basil sprig
juice of 1 lemon
little lemon zest
about 3 teaspoons ground cinnamon

Place the apples and pineapple in a pot with just enough water to simmer them in. Tuck in the basil sprig. Cover and simmer until tender. Add the lemon juice, zest and cinnamon and simmer for 2 minutes. Put aside.

Crumble topping
2 tablespoons each of:
sunflower seeds
wheat germ flakes
sesame seed
finely chopped pecan nuts
desiccated coconut
3 tablespoons each of:
soft butter
bran

Mix all the filling ingredients well. Spoon the fruit into an ovenproof dish, discarding the basil sprig. Sprinkle with cinnamon. Sprinkle the crumble over the fruit and bake at 180°C for 10-15 minutes, or until the topping becomes golden brown. Serve hot.

RHUBARB AND SPICY BASIL FOOL
Serves 6-8

1 kg rhubarb, cut into 2 cm pieces
3 perennial or camphor basil sprigs
3-4 eggs whisked with 2 tablespoons cornflour
3-4 tablespoons honey
2 teaspoons grated ginger root
2 cups milk mixed with
100 ml thick cream or cottage cheese

Boil the rhubarb in a little water with the basil until tender. Whisk the eggs and cornflour with the honey and ginger until thick and creamy. Warm the milk and cream or cottage cheese and add a little of the egg mixture, whisking well. Keep on a low heat, gradually adding the rest of the egg mixture. Stir well with a wooden spoon until it forms a thick custard. Set aside and cool. Remove the basil from the rhubarb mixture and stir in the custard. Pour into individual serving dishes, chill and top with whipped cream, dust with a little powdered ginger and decorate with a rosette of tiny camphor basil leaves.

CAMPHOR BASIL SHERRY MELON

Serves 6
This is a stunning dish to serve at the end of a rich meal.

1 spanspek, peeled and cubed, or formed into balls
1 honeydew melon, peeled and cubed, or formed into balls
½ cup medium sweet sherry
½ cup brown sugar mixed with 1 tablespoon camphor
  or cinnamon basil, finely chopped

Arrange the melon attractively in a flat glass dish. Slowly dribble a little sherry over it, then sprinkle with the sugar and basil mixture. Decorate with borage and violet flowers and little flowering sprigs of camphor or cinnamon basil.

❧ HANDY HINT
Three sprigs of basil steeped in a bottle of wine for 6 hours makes a wonderful tonic that can be taken daily.

Drinks

Although basil is not often used in teas and drinks, I have never forgotten a glorious basil drink I once had after over-indulging in a sumptuous — but rather rich and spicy — Mediterranean-style dinner. The basil drink was wonderfully soothing and ensured excellent digestion. Since then, I have often used basil as a night cap. Lemon basil, the perennial basils, camphor basil or cinnamon basil are best, and if you were to enjoy a basil tea on its own, you would make it of any of these as well.

BASIL TEA
Serves 8

¼ cup fresh basil leaves and flowering heads
1 cup boiling water

Pour the boiling water over the basil and leave to stand for 5 minutes. Strain. Serve hot in coffee cups.

Use this tea as the base for the basil after dinner drink.

Basil after dinner drink

Serves 8

3 cups boiling water
1 cup basil leaves and flowering sprigs
1 cinnamon stick
2 cups apple juice
½ cup dry sherry
½ cup brown sugar

Pour the boiling water over the basil leaves and cinnamon stick. Stand for 5-10 minutes. Strain. Add the apple juice and sherry. Warm briefly with the brown sugar. Stir with a cinnamon stick. Serve hot.

Basil aphrodisiac wine

Why not sip a glass of this wonderful wine with someone special after that basil bath (see page 47)!

It will also help mental fatigue, depression and burnout.

1 bottle red wine
a few sprigs dark opal or lemon basil
8 red rose petals
1 stick cinnamon
1-2 tablespoons honey or brown sugar

Uncork your favourite red wine and push into it a few sprigs of your favourite basil, the rose petals, cinnamon, and honey or brown sugar. Replace the cork and shake well. Leave to mature for 2 days in a dark cupboard. Give it a daily shake.

BASIL SANGRIA

Serves 8

This is a rather medieval drink which is wonderful served hot in midwinter and is helpful for chills, coughs and colds. It is equally delicious served chilled with crushed ice at a midsummer garden party.

1 cup basil leaves and sprigs (spicy globe, cinnamon basil
*   or perennial basil are nicest here)*
2 cups boiling water
10 cloves
1 stick cinnamon
10 allspice berries
4 cups good red wine
2 cups grape juice
lemon or naartjie slices

Pour the boiling water over the basil and the spices. Leave to cool, then strain. Add the wine and the grape juice and stir well. At this point you may either warm it or chill it.

In winter I serve it hot in wine glasses with naartjie slices dipped in brown sugar or in summer chilled with lemon slices dipped in castor sugar.

Decorate with a basil leaf floating on the lemon or naartjie slices, or use a flowering sprig to gently stir it.

HINT: To avoid cracking the glass, pour the hot sangria over a teaspoon standing in the glass.

BASIL PARTY PUNCH
Serves 8-10

2 litres boiling water
2 cups lemon or cinnamon basil leaves and sprigs
1 litre mango or peach juice
1 litre litchi or grape juice
crushed ice
thin slices of fruit
basil leaves

Pour the boiling water over the basil leaves and sprigs. Stand until cool, then strain. Add mango or peach juice and litchi or grape juice. Chill. Add crushed ice, thin slices of fruit and basil leaves to float on top. Serve in tall glasses or a traditional punch bowl with cups.

BASIL WINTER WARMER
Serves 1

1 cup boiling water
¼ cup basil sprigs
4 cloves
1 piece cinnamon
1 tablespoon lemon juice
2 teaspoons honey

Pour boiling water over the basil sprigs, cloves and cinnamon. Stand for 5 minutes. Strain. Stir in the lemon juice and honey. Sip slowly.

Sauces and dressings

In my lectures I have often encountered chefs who are surprised to discover that the culinary uses of basil are not limited to sauces, pesto and salsa. They are astonished when I suggest using it with fish, in soup and in desserts. Nevertheless, this section is for all those chefs who like to keep basil in its 'rightful' place!

PESTO SAUCE

I have made countless variations over the years, but this is my favourite recipe for this classic Genoese sauce. Use it on all types of pasta, baked potatoes and add it to soups, casseroles and grills, or try spreading a little on crusty brown bread and eating it with tomato soup.

4 cups fresh sweet basil leaves (or perennial sweet basil)
2-3 cloves garlic, peeled
sea salt to taste
4 tablespoons pine nuts (or chopped walnuts)
5–6 tablespoons virgin olive oil
4 tablespoons Parmesan cheese

In a large pestle and mortar pound the basil leaves with the garlic. Add the salt, pine nuts and a little of the olive oil, pounding all the time. Add the cheese alternately with the oil until a smooth paste is formed.

BASIL OIL

1 cup fresh sweet basil, chopped
olive oil or sunflower oil to fill the bottle
3-4 garlic cloves, peeled and trimmed, or 2 chillies (optional) or cayenne
  peppers or 1 teaspoon peppercorns
little coarse sea salt

Pack the basil into the bottle, add the garlic, chillies, peppers or peppercorns and salt, and fill up with the oil. Shake well. Store in the fridge for at least 2 days before using.

This oil is delicious with stir fries, grills, as a marinade with lemon juice added, or as a salad dressing.

> ❧ HANDY HINT
> In Japan, India and West
> Africa several basil species
> are used to treat chronic
> bronchitis, flu, coughs and
> to bring down fevers.

Basil salsa

This is a delicious tomato and basil sauce that tastes marvellous on just about anything: pasta, potatoes, fish, grills, good old 'stywe pap', cold meats, baked beans, rice dishes and chicken dishes. Versatile and tasty, it is best made fresh every time, but it can be kept in the fridge for up to a week.

2 large onions, chopped
1 cup celery, finely chopped
6 large tomatoes, skinned and chopped
2 green peppers, chopped
1 cup basil leaves, chopped
½ cup brown sugar
sea salt and black pepper to taste
1 cayenne pepper, chopped if you like it hot
3 tablespoons basil oil

Lightly brown the onions and celery in the oil. Stir in the tomatoes and green peppers, and simmer while stirring frequently. Add the rest of the ingredients and stir for 5 minutes. (You can add about 1 cup water thickened with 3 teaspoons cornflour at this stage should you want a thicker salsa.)

Taste and adjust salt if necessary. Serve piping hot.

BASIL SALAD VINEGAR

4 or 5 fresh basil sprigs
1 bottle white grape vinegar

Press the basil sprigs into the bottle of vinegar. Stand in the sun for 10-14 days. During that time, strain and discard the basil sprigs and replace them with fresh ones at least 3 times, or until you get the flavour you like. Finally, strain and add an attractive fresh sprig, cork and label.

Use as a salad dressing, in stir fries and stews.

VARIATIONS: Add cayenne pepper, coriander seeds, allspice berries or garlic, or a combination, to the final bottle, as their tastes are very strong.

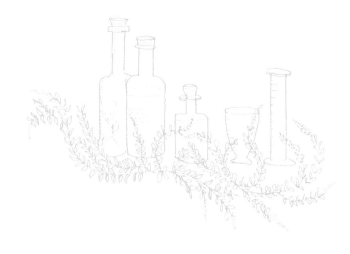

Basil in cosmetics

ॐ

With the importance of natural ingredients being increasingly recognised, basil will without doubt be used more and more in both medicine and the cosmetics industry in the new century.

As toxins in the environment and in the food we eat take their toll on health, scientists are looking at basil's remarkable properties as a detoxifier with new respect. Its active ingredients like linalool, camphor, estragol, geraniol, borneol, eugenol, cineol, pinene, phenolic acids and vitamins A and C make it an important anti-bacterial agent and stimulant for cell regeneration.

Basil in various forms has long been recognised as an effective home treatment for skin conditions such as acne, oiliness and dryness, and for fatigue and aching muscles and feet.

Basil bath oil

This is excellent for fatigue, insomnia, stress, migraine, colds and flu and is particularly useful in treating winter chills and building up the immune system.

1 bottle almond oil
several sprigs of basil (camphor basil or perennial pink or
    white basil are nicest here)

Submerge the basil in the oil in a double boiler and boil gently with the lid on for 20 minutes. Leave to cool, strain, bottle and add a sprig of dried basil for quick identification.
    Add 2 teaspoons to the bath, and relax.

Basil foot soak

This is an excellent treatment for aching feet and is superb for deodorising the feet and softening corns and callouses.

2 litres boiling water
6 large sprigs camphor basil
½ cup basil vinegar
1 cup Epsom salts

Pour the boiling water over the fresh basil and leave to cool until pleasantly warm. Remove the basil, add the vinegar and Epsom salts, and mix well. Either soak the feet in this, or wrap a face cloth soaked in it around the feet. Relax for 10- 15 minutes. Rinse the feet and briskly towel dry. This same mixture can be used again once or twice. Store in a corked bottle.

BASIL BATH AND HAIR VINEGAR

This is particularly helpful for oily hair and skin. Just add a little to the rinsing water or use a pad of cotton wool squeezed out in cold water and then dipped into the vinegar and wipe gently over the face and neck. Its soothing astringent qualities make it an excellent skin treatment for problem skins. I like camphor basil or dark opal basil best for this recipe.

1 bottle apple cider vinegar
approximately 6 sprigs basil, including flowers
10 cloves
5 allspice berries

Push the allspice berries and the basil into the vinegar. Cork well and stand in the sun for 2 weeks. During that time, strain, discard the old basil, and add fresh basil to the vinegar (the same cloves and allspice berries can be used each time). Do this up to 4 times, until you get the strength you require. Finally strain out all the spices and basil sprigs. Pour into a pretty bottle, add a fresh sprig for quick identification and cork well.

BASIL CREAM FOR ACHING MUSCLES

I've found this indispensable for aches and pains and cramps and make it frequently for the athletes who come for a good massage cream. It soothes stiff, cold feet too, so use it generously and frequently.

1 cup good aqueous cream
1 cup fresh chopped camphor basil or
*   sacred basil leaves and flowering heads*
1 teaspoon basil aromatherapy oil

Gently simmer the cream and the basil in a double boiler for 20 minutes. Press the basil leaves under the cream frequently. Stand aside and cool. Strain and mix in 1 teaspoon of the basil aromatherapy oil (this last ingredient can be left out if you feel the cream is strong enough, or you could repeat the 20 minute simmering with a new cup of fresh leaves). Store in a sterilised screw-top glass jar.

> **❧ HANDY HINT**
> To dry basil, wash several sprigs, pat dry, place on brown paper in the shade and turn daily until crisp.

BASIL FACE STEAMER

Through the years I've experimented with a wide range of herbal ingredients to find the ideal astringent cleansing steamer, and this combination of herbs is my favourite. Basil is the main ingredient and I find either the perennial pink or white flowered basil or camphor basil nicest here. Vary the other herbs in smaller quantities according to preference.

This steamer will soften the skin, enabling stubborn blackheads to be gently squeezed out. It helps clear acne and refines the skin.

Do not use facial steamers if you have thread veins.

1 large bowl boiling water
basil sprigs
yarrow, spearmint, lemon verbena or sage

Submerge the basil sprigs in the water with any of the other herbs you like. Make a towel tent over your head and gently lower your face over the steaming bowl, keeping your eyes closed. Allow the steam to condense and drip off. Inhale deeply. (Basil will help clear the lungs and sinuses too.) After several minutes, pat dry and carefully and very gently ease out blackheads or whiteheads. Dab your skin with a little rose water once you've cooled down. Leave make-up off for a day, to give your skin a chance to heal and breathe.

BASIL MOISTURISING CREAM

This is excellent as a night cream or for very dry skin. I use it not only on my face, but over rough heels and elbows and on my legs during winter. Massaged into the cuticles it helps prevent nails from chipping and breaking.

1 tablespoon lanolin
3 tablespoons almond oil
2 tablespoons strong camphor basil infusion (see below)
1 teaspoon beeswax (available from a chemist)
2 tablespoons aqueous cream
1 teaspoon vitamin E oil

Make the basil infusion by pouring 1 cup of boiling water over ¾ cup of fresh camphor basil sprigs. Leave to draw for about 20 minutes, then strain.

Warm everything except for the vitamin E oil in a double boiler for 10 minutes. Stir carefully to ensure everything is well mixed. Add the vitamin E oil once you remove the mixture from the heat. This will act as a preservative as well as smooth wrinkles and heal blemishes. After 10-15 minutes, pour the cream into a sterilised glass jar with a screw-top lid.

Store the cream in a sealed jar in the fridge during summer to keep it fresh.

Medicinal uses of basil

Owing to its remarkable healing properties, basil is being used more and more in medicine. It has proved to be useful in the treatment of a wide variety of ailments, and in many countries basil is a recognised ingredient in certain patented medicines. In India a basil sprig is rubbed between the hands and the lovely aroma inhaled to give people sattua, enlightenment and harmony. For home remedy purposes, basil can be helpful for the same conditions, in various forms, such as tea, a wash, gargle, compress, decoction or oil, or simply eaten in its raw state.

Remember to always consult your doctor before starting a home treatment.

⁂ Basil tea
Basil tea will work wonders for *stress-related diseases* such as *peptic ulcers* and *migraines, coughs, tonsillitis, mouth infections, hypertension, delayed menstruation, intestinal worms, palpitations, indigestion* and *stimulating lactation in nursing mothers.* Basil tea taken after eating very rich food will help to lessen its effects on the liver. Some health experts recommend drinking a cup of basil tea after radiation therapy or chemotherapy, as it *alleviates nausea* and the fragrance does much to soothe the patient. Taken daily, basil tea is considered an excellent treatment for acne and other skin disorders.

¼ cup fresh basil leaves (sweet basil or perennial sweet basil)
1 cup boiling water

Pour the boiling water over the basil leaves, stand for 5 minutes, then strain. Sip slowly.

⁂ Basil invigorating spray
Sprayed into a room this will help revitalise *frayed nerves* and *mental fatigue.* A few drops dabbed onto a handkerchief and inhaled will invigorate you and make you feel more *alert.*

1 teaspoon basil essential oil
1 litre water

Dilute the basil essential oil and decant it into a bottle with a spray gun.

ᘔ Basil vinegar

Basil vinegar diluted with water (2 teaspoons vinegar in $\frac{1}{2}$ glass water) will relieve *nausea, colic* and *digestive upsets*. I always travel with a little bottle of this and add it as a matter of course to the drinking water to ensure that I have no tummy upsets. It also helps with *insomnia, stress* and *tension*. Use it as a gargle (2-3 teaspoons in a glass of water) for *sore throats* and *mouth infections*.

3 or 4 basil sprigs (sweet basil, lemon basil or dark opal basil)
1 bottle apple cider vinegar

Press the basil sprigs into the bottle of vinegar and leave it to stand in a warm place for 2 days. Remove the spent sprigs and add fresh ones. Repeat this for extra strength. Finally, add a fresh sprig for identification.

ᘔ Basil insect bite soother

Crushed basil leaves will soothe *insect bites* and *stings* and get rid of *corns* and *planter warts* if they are gently and frequently rubbed over the area. A basil leaf warmed in hot water is an excellent compress over *boils, infected sores* and *bites*, and fresh basil leaves can also be added to the bath to soothe *rashes, grazes* and *itchy, infected bites* and *stings*. Alternatively, use a basil wash as a lotion for the same purpose, applying frequently.

ᘔ Basil wash

2 cups fresh basil leaves and sprigs
2 litres boiling water

Pour the boiling water over the basil, stand until cool, then strain.

❧ Basil decoction
Basil is an effective treatment for *psoriasis of the scalp, scalp infections* and *scaly, weeping eczemas*. Use this decoction as a final rinse after shampooing and comb into the hair frequently, or dab it onto the eczema and sores. It can also be added to the bath to invigorate those suffering from *fatigue, nervous exhaustion* and *debilitating stress* and *depression*. Washing the feet with this decoction was also an old-fashioned remedy for *corns* and *planter warts*.

1 cup fresh basil leaves
2 litres water

Boil the basil leaves in the water for 10 minutes. Strain and cool until pleasantly warm.

❧ As a *breath freshener* basil is excellent! Just chew a fresh leaf or two, as the Italians do, after a meal rich in garlic and spices.

❧ Aromatherapy
The uses of basil in aromatherapy are diverse: as an *antispasmodic, tonic* and *diuretic,* for *flatulence, menstrual irregularities* and *menopausal symptoms, fatigue, insomnia, stress, migraine, colds, flu, viral infections, palpitations, weepiness* and *depression*. Basil oil has long been used by aromatherapists in an almond or sweet oil base. The presence of estragol (or methyl chavicol) in basil has been known to cause a reaction to sensitive skins, however, and this has led to the search for a species of basil without this substance. *Ocimum sanctum,* or sacred basil, seems to contain the least of this substance of all the species (although this may be affected by where the basil is grown, as in very hot, humid areas it has been found to have less).

Basil as a companion plant

Over the years I have come to appreciate the remarkable benefits of companion planting. I've proved it in the trial gardens here at the Herbal Centre and I am constantly astonished at the protection plants are able to give to one another, particularly in times of adverse weather conditions such as heavy rains, drought or intense heat.

As a rule you cannot have too much basil in the garden. All varieties of it, from the sturdy perennials to the tender annuals, make successful companion plants.

◆ Basil repels fruit fly around *apricot, peach and pear trees,* and sacred basil seems to protect *quinces* from being stung.

◆ *Asparagus* does well with basil and tomatoes planted nearby. The asparagus produces a substance called asparagin, which repels the tomatoes' arch enemy, nematodes, and the basil keeps aphids away from both!

◆ Basil is loved by bees, so plant it near *melissa, hyssop and winter and summer savory.* All of them will burst with growth.

◆ *Parsley* flourishes near basil and tomatoes too, with all three free of aphids and white fly.

◆ Surrounded by basil and sage, *grape vines* will produce prolific, sweet fruit.

◆ *Sweetpeas* and *garden peas* planted in winter do well with the perennial basils planted near them and will be kept free of mildew when the spring weather warms up.

SUCCESSFUL VEGETABLE GARDEN COMPANIONS

radish, basil, tomato, parsley • beans, basil, lettuce, chives • beetroot, basil, strawberry, winter savory • gem squash, basil, onions, celery • carrots, basil, mealies, borage • green pepper, basil, mustard, brinjal • butter lettuce, basil, bush beans, spring onions

CNA WESTGATE
WESTGATE SHOPPING COMPLEX
WESTGATE, HARARE
TEL : 332615
Cash Sale
CASHIER : RDUA

1157625 07/01/1998 07:42:06

cription   Price
----
cription   Price
KS   155.75

AL   :   155.75
ES TAX (INC.)   :   23.20

    PAID   :   200.00
    CHANGE   :   44.25

       CASH

THANK YOU FOR SHOPPING WITH US

Natural insecticides

From around the fourteenth century basil was used as a strewing herb.

The pungent, clove-like oil in the perennial basil leaves is a powerful insect repellent. Flies and mosquitoes particularly dislike basil and on hot summer days when the flies are innumerable, I bring great bunches of fresh basil into the kitchen to stand in jugs of water, or I rub it into wooden tables and along windowsills. The perennial basils are best for this purpose, owing to their pungent, camphor-like scent.

At summer braais I have basil fly whisks tied with raffia at each chair, and crush the leaves lightly from time to time to keep the flies and mosquitoes at bay. A little basil oil dropped onto an outdoor candle also keeps mosquitoes away.

Big bunches of fresh basil and khakibos or rue tied and hung in stables keep flies from worrying the horses. I also rub the stable doors well with the leaves early in the morning to release the oils.

BASIL SPRAY FOR WHITE FLY, APHIDS, RED SPIDER AND CUTWORMS

½ *bucket mixed fresh perennial basil or camphor basil sprigs,*
  khakibos, rue and tansy
1 *bucket boiling water*
1 *cup soap powder*

Pour the boiling water over the herbs and stand overnight. Next morning strain, discard the spent herbs and stir in the soap powder. Mix well, and use as a spray or splash on for white fly, aphids and red spider or water around plants to deter cutworms. An oak leaf mulch will deter cutworms further, as they cannot cross it.

BASIL AND RUE EXTRACT FOR ANTS' HOLES

½ *bucket mixed perennial basil or camphor basil sprigs,*
  rue leaves and seed heads
1 *bucket water*
½ - 1 *cup Jeyes fluid*
1 *cup soap powder*

Boil the basil and rue for 10 minutes in the water. Allow to cool. Strain and add the Jeyes fluid and soap powder. Mix well. Pour down holes and between cracks on paving.

Basil floor and furniture polish

My grandmother taught me to make this polish, and it is an excellent way to keep ants, fishmoths and flies out of the house.

CAUTION: Be extremely careful when warming the polish — hot polish is extremely dangerous. Keep children and pets out of the room.

1 tin polish
1 cup roughly broken perennial basil leaves and flowers
basil essential oil (optional)

Warm a tin of your favourite polish by placing the tin in a pot of boiling water until the polish melts. Add the basil leaves and flowers, and let it simmer for 20 minutes. Remove the basil — the liquid polish will be well scented by now. (Here you could add a little basil essential oil for extra strength if you have some.)

Allow the polish to set and harden, then use it as you would any normal polish. The room will smell marvellous and there will be no sign of a fly or mosquito!

Basil window wash

½ bucket perennial basil sprigs and leaves (camphor basil is best)
1 bucket water
1 cup soap powder

Boil up the basil leaves and sprigs in the water for 10 minutes. Cool and strain. Add the soap powder. Use this strong brew as a window or paintwork wash — the flies will not come near the fragrant surfaces!

INDEX